HORIZON

Kritin Jain

BookLeaf Publishing

India | USA | UK

Presentation by *BookLeaf Publishing*

Web: www.bookleafpub.com

E-mail: info@bookleafpub.com

ISBN: 9789363316294

First edition 2024

After all

It's

WOVEN IN MY SOUL

Kritin Jain is an eighteen-year-old who intricately weaves themes of captivity and compassion into poetry. Brought up in the lake-city and now hustling in urban areas, Kritin finds reasons to calm the demons held back by people. He untangles his own mind while seeking to untangle the lives of others through his words. He craves to bridge the gap between his heart and mind and that of his readers, aiming to make this world a heartier place, one poem at a time.

From the author,

It is a truth universally acknowledged that a person in love and a person in pain is someone of a slave to music, thoughts and words. The immediate forms of complete and utter expression and elements to curb the illimited delight and to numb the anguish.

In order to get the most out of this book, the author suggests:

Turn on music

Grab hold of a memory or a fairytale

Help yourself with a pen and paper

And let's dive

Into a thousand minds.

Contents

Introduction

the reason behind horizon

Love can be elusive to name but words can be equally simpler to define, everything we have ever felt and anything that tears us apart. This book was written for a lost mind and an eager heart.

The author believes that horizon is within us, as we always long for things in life, we move further towards fate. Horizon is the point where the earth and the sky intersect, henceforth where destiny lies. All of us crave to acquire the things we desire but fate has its card and it can be a different end to an exquisite plan. That's what it's felt by the seaside where one can see the gorgeous evening line and not the end.

Hoping each and every reader finds their set of emotions here and is consoled by the words written by someone very much like them, broken, lover, fighter, and everything in between.

.

till the horizon and back
the mist that whispers a lullaby
and the drops that flows glory
let's be away from all
all mankind that ignites love
and seeks to live on lies
we have one paradise we can chase
let's be away love
far away

.

Far from silence

Partially consumed by oaths and demons

.

the first half was just the beginning
i didn't realise until i looked back
to see that you were fading
the first half was dust
our rhythm was failing
from your heart
and in my mind
the oaths had me draining
the demons got me: haunting

.

if i have actually made peace
with the fact that you are gone
why do i see myself
showing people the person
i am absolutely not
~what have you done to me

when i called you my night
the light
weren't the stars
but the dazzling city before my eyes
as midnight came
the lights seemed to vanish
and you started to fade

it's okay, that someone took over the place in your heart that once was mine. i don't hate you for that. i only fear that if the new one has the capacity to consume the pain that you may pour upon him like you did on me. not everyone can write in abundance so vacantly, like i did.

if i forget you
i'll forget what you did too
so instead let me remember
and suffer your loss
so, i don't make the same mistakes again

i am sorry for the misunderstandings
from i need time for myself
to you wouldn't understand me
i am sorry i never understood
you could numb my pain
like turbulence fell and i missed your call
i should've known you were there
gradual steps make it better
maybe i had put the ladder upside down

like the mornings perished into darkness
the night will go by and by
the moon as it goes
takes away my essence
and the universe
like it was never mine

only if i could forget
the faint cries of our laughter
in the old classroom
where we met for the first time
teased each other till the bell rang
ate lunch together in the most innocent way
and maybe only there we will stay

together
in the past

in the valleys deep down
till its bed no voice did reach
the echoes did scream
till the clouds and back
escapism was never the key

hiding behind my mistakes
i watch him everyday
when he passes by my house
with a false smirk on his face and wet eyes
he wishes to look at me
always does he look at the narrow road
where i held his hands for a long walk
i watch him everyday
hoping for a different look on his face
a look that has forgotten me

i developed some feelings for you
but in the back of my memory
other feelings haunted me too
same as the last time i saw someone with my
loving eyes

when i see the night-sky
i wish to be whole again
but the moon never seems to be

never more than half
it appears as if

it's been emptier than me

why do i write? they ask

for the person i want to write for
doesn't want to read me
i write in grief about love
and in happiness about pain
for the people and their ones
who are appreciated
~finding affirmations in rejections

always a goodbye on the way
just before....
one dinner
one coffee
one movie
one walk between all this
one flower
one proposal
one hug
one love
the manifestation that turned into a
heartbreak

the poetry in me is a replacement
to the breath you took away
and the words that filled my home
is the vacancy you ever made

raindrops witnessed
the first time
hailstorm the last
yet it had the hints of the rain
the drops of love did surpass

i know we didn't survive the heats of march
and that we lost touch
by some nautical miles each year
i spent the years before and years after
falling for you
trying to gather the fog we turned into
i am so weak
for my strength tries to reach you
alas, the next day you said,
"love for me never existed for you"

sun?
moon?
rain?
fire?
no
we were snowflakes
wind that turned us into ice
ice that was formed to melt
you were right when you told me
we are nothing but elements

the final act
and that was it for the perfect-two
with a shiver, she held him
the heavens poured
her eyes wept more than the clouds that day
and his heart shattered a little more

a single-handed wound is not a scar given by someone else, it is most likely that you will endure the pain yourself. the ones who left are long gone and the dusk begins the night, all paths to change the fact will prove to be a dead end.

if you have never experienced heartbreak
have you ever loved anyone?
to the extent
of feeling too much?

perhaps in the beginning of time
when my heart had beaten this quick
it was when i confessed to you

now it's finally beating the same way
when you are not where you used to be

and you were supposed to be
different

i shouldn't have loved every piece of you
now every bit of it hurts me too

but somehow you always stayed: subliminal
and yet after those memories
the new 'hey' had many lies
it was past a thousand years
since that one year

sometimes you are just sad, with no poetry attached, no music to tolerate, no skies, no seas, no one to listen to, no escape, no safe place, no hopeless prayers, nothing. and those are the particular times when you are just trying to talk properly for once at home or waiting for someone's message desperately or fighting with that one person you actually trust the most.

you have to gulp that pain, because even your eyes need some emotions to gather up and cry someday. and the tears that shed, take away most of the pain.

does the silence really tick us off or the chaos?
is the void lonelier or the screams?
are the memories raiding your mind?
or are you stuck between
the haunting demons and the overwhelming
kind?

i picked up a log
to cut it into half
i raised the axe with all my strength
and slashed it oddly
call it a chaos

i still did not feel satisfied
i had my heart pounding
louder than ever

i still felt
i was stronger than just one log to pile
and my pain was sharper than the rustic worn
knife

~what i meant to kill never died, those thoughts
still hit me when the clock hits midnight

we were imperfectly perfect until you tore us
apart and now, we are perfectly imperfect

the first half

a person in love
is in passion to write about heartbreak
crippled by their own minds
fearing the terrific tides

feeling so soundly incomplete
and so poorly out of time

the other half

but a person in possession of a heart
other than theirs
is incapable of writing about the worst way
fears are buried by reality
reality is crippled into mist
leaving it to hope that it may not alter
because they know
there is no weeping now
for a lie like another day
and a day with another lie

now that you have made up your mind, i plead
you not to change your decision and make me
like yourself—disturbed and broken.

a thousand screams in my dreams
that call out your name
when i wake up
i know you are somebody else's
but the crave of seeing you never goes
and the fear of looking in your eyes remains
because,
eyes ~~don't lie~~ speak
far more than your mind wants
yet a little less than your heart needs
a thousand screams in my dreams
that stop me from loving you

i was a wanderlust for love
forsaken heart, yearning kind
only if it was beyond my mind

and at the bridge over river seine
where i locked our names
by the city's lights
i hoped our future never dries
the eiffel tower that testifies my love
but how would i know
the next year it would be yours to hope
for someone else
just next to mine

you choose to settle for the moon
waiting for it your whole day
and still, it leaves you
crying away

please be different
i will take over your demons
but i don't want the same pain
twice

little did i know
the previous year
it was like a cave i walked into
where my own voice haunted me
i was trapped far beyond reality
screams that called out no one
but my past and the unhappened fear
how could i move on?
how could i run?
when my demons and i were one

she was loud enough
to be heard by everyone

except him
her dying cries of cure
felt like a bruise to him
when it started to heal
she was already a past

your lies were the crack
my mistakes were the drop
and we were the splinter

and you let her go
and you call that love
and it means an eternity without you
and you'll be unhappy

because you let her go
because you say you love her
because you want an eternity of her memory
because you want her happy

i would hold on instead
i'd call that love
i'll make us a sacred timeline
i'll call it our 'happily ever after'

it was an act
started, written, and ended by me
but my subconscious reads it everyday
hoping for a different end
it was an act
i cannot forget
it was an end
i cannot change

you listen to those songs
like it's your first time
and by verse you speak to someone else
not remembering once it was yours and mine
the songs you liked
and that i liked you
i sung for you in an awful voice
but for me those tunes left
and my guitar that did strum for you
and so, did you know
or probably you took it from me
for you and yours
and as you listen to them now
i hope to be playing them for you
somewhere back in your memory

i fell
consciously
fell in my own mind
i saw the past for real one more time
i saw the fantasies and realities
that pulled me back
not letting me stay alive
i wished to fly again

you say,
there is a thin line between love and hate
but it's much more perhaps

a line between a song and a lament
hope and regret
attachment and crumble
go away and come back
i miss you and i mourn you
you are forgiven and forgotten
remember, there is a line still
a thin line
bye and goodbye
come back and farewell

the mountains spirited
that hide behind the nasty clouds
heavenly crisp winds
that take away my anguish
it forced me
to leave the lost me
for the fogged them

it hurts me as much as it hurts you

when you cry for someone
i am dying to meet you
when likeness is an echo
reaching back to me before it reaches you
you will never know
what my thoughts thought of you
it hurts me as much as it hurts you

my friend once asked me
why do poets romanticise pain?

why not?
when all you think about is someone who is
not with you
or all you ignore are the songs on the radio
and what grief offers is much more relaxing
than wounds
because you bleed love in grief
and pain in scars
and everything that gets you closer to them
makes you feel apart

isn't this awfully lovable?
that night can never perish
so, you have to learn
how to love the stars

i imagined our saturday nights
when it rained, it poured
by the waffle stand we sit close
under the umbrella we share
but

afar, i stood…
looking at my hoped destiny
staring at my imagination
across the road

by the waffle stand they sit close
when it rained it poured
i imagined our saturday nights
but he was your reality

afar i stood
that shattering sight
you and your one
a perfect little night

and when i see someone
i lose my words to the soil
not realising until i look back
i have been giving them
to the wrong people every time
and now it feels like
talking to the noon at night
perhaps the same as looking at the sea
with no reflecting sunlight

i thought it was okay....
that we were drifting apart everyday
hopefully by time we will heal
mistakes forgotten and forgiven
and i would pull you back in no time
the distance between us
did cover the wounded path
i thought it was okay...
for me to ask you to stay
but by then,
you were already a lightyear away

a bed of artificial grass
to lay over our unreal love
to stop the reminders of the place
where i sat to talk to you over the phone
and walked like i had days in my pocket
spring, summer, autumn
we lost track of time
a bed of artificial grass
because we couldn't survive before the cold
winds
and so that i don't remember you
once again in the heats of march

the pain i invited
for the freedom of mine
that is yours somehow
the hopes in me that i lighted in you
i feel like a ghost now
bit by bit that you pulled from me
hence, i am an empty ocean
my heart was never broken
but it's definitely torn now

when it's time for farewell
understanding can't heal
conversations can't heal
acceptance can't heal
and promises can't heal
forgiving will never be forgetting
and faith will never be trust
eyes will lie more than they speak
and mind will ring shatters of love
wounds and bruises with bandages
that might hide but never well enough
there is no healing when it's...
THE END

Eclipse and silhouettes

Symphony of emotion, passion, and touch

.

we collided like it was meant to be

a symphony of emotion, passion and touch

that brings dusk and dawn together

like the sun and moon in one frame

casting a shadow that witnesses our meet

and then you go away

waiting for the eclipse one more time

when our silhouette speaks more than the

nighttime

.

your heart skipped a beat
you call it a blank space?
is it really a vacancy
or a void where there once was someone's name
there's an empty vase in my room
distorted polaroids
and a lost scent
letters by no one
summer with no sun
monsoon and no rain
tables of my classroom
scraped with a compass
i love____and there once was someone's name
~ *pastime*

i could scroll through my whole playlist
741 reasons to find you
one word from each song
to make a new verse
for you

that night
when the seashore and i were friends
i gifted my grief to the water that takes it
away from me
with a tune it passes away my guilt
and drowns my anxiety beneath
the night acknowledges my return
for everyone appreciates and leaves
that night
when the seashore and i were friends
the universe wanted to talk to me

all the kinds did they have
boundless of them
the farthest section
the last corner
and i picked you
the only anthology

he was so lost in oceans
she was his mermaid
and that explained

a thousand poems for you
and still an infinite remains incomplete
it's like with my bare hands
i hold the place where the clouds meet the sky
and touching the point where the sea and sun
meet
for that someone i lay all my words
like a constellation of stars
how could i ever end what i started for you
even before you entered my life
and left a million times
you gave me love, hope and scars
and that was enough for me

she is the emergence of light
and the allure of darkness
she is the queen
to my abandoned palace

if you can completely and utterly fall for love
and at the same time
loathe it every inch
cherish it and be scared of it
then you can write
you can sing
you can play
you can smile
you can cry
you can live

you tell me,
we are perfectly different from the rest
i feel we are antiquely apart from them
the lie-like dust that keeps us safely lost
the letters that keep us preserved
for eternity locked away
with rhythms from past, i dance with you
in our eyes, the unsevered link
crisply folded beneath the lie-like rust
we are perfectly antique
and differently apart from them

and till the end of time
he still had her
in the files that kept hidden
in those clumsy handwritten letters
in the memory of the blue dress, she walked in
that day

sometimes i just wish i would have never asked
the meaning of 'crush' when i was fourteen

sometimes i just wish i would have never asked
the meaning of 'love' when i was seventeen

sometimes i just wish i would have never asked
the meaning of 'forever' when i was twenty

too soon to face reality

oh heart of mine
know her like i have known you in life
be a little more gentle
not a lot like kind
love her like a petal
but let her not consume you overtime

the first half

i'm not surprised to see you once again
after the first time
and before it could happen twice
like the impossible thunder that led my ghost
to yours
just to meet you in a land unknown
in my head like a play
or manifesting a fair encounter like a tale

i'm not surprised that we are sitting in the
same place
years after where we met
on the edge of the pool
where i ended my day
and you just started your night
talking to the moon like you were welcoming a
new life

the second half

as for me i searched for a vacant space
in the heavens where you looked at
hoping for a different end
when you welcome a new life every night
by talking to me everyday

they all called you a mischance
well, my heart would take those chances again
...... until this thing's over

when a boy loved her
it was when
he had his complete heart with him
he was innocent and eager
and kind with his gestures

when he became a man
he had once lost his self-respect
he had once cried for a better self
and prayed once for a merciful life
but when that man loved her
it was like the divine upheld the delicate
strings
that held them together
it was innocently passionate
and eagerly patient

she told him
she loves the night
the sea without blues
the darkest sky
the shiniest stars
the silent type

he stole everything she ever loved

and gifted her music
of the peace sound she liked
and poetry of the words she gazed upon
day and night

as kids when we painted together
on the white walls outside your house
from the figures and sketches we wouldn't
understand
to art that only we knew
the paint and brush and i were gone
you left the blanks for me
in faith that i would come
to fill out the blanks and make us a story
to colour the walls and make it a home

~stay

i might be the 97% of the water
surrounding you, trying to be compatible
but you are the 3% to me
only reason to stay alive

after
the evening we met
did you think of me after going home?
did my eyes settle into yours?
or did the aroma tag along?
did you ask about me to your friends?
or looking for just one more coincidence
any cries were there....?
to meet me just once again?
~hope

perhaps fate was the colour
that dropped upon us
turning our scenery
into an abstract

there is this knot in our minds
of the memory that's never happened before
it's called craving
not imagining
craving
into crystals by a parallel way
not yet a memory
and it's gone away
just like it never happened before

my catalina?
heather?
valerie?
hope?
my endless search for the perfect one
the search ended
when i called out that name
it was of my daughter

i didn't believe in that one emotion
until it gave me all others
love is anonymous
love is _________

you were the scars of 6 a.m.
that turned you to lavender
and then to peach
the midnight rain behind which you hide
you were the hopes and dreams
what will i do without you

letters are for souls
it's not yours to remember
after you take it away from your eyes
perhaps with a distant voice the words reach
our souls back
reminding us how they remain worthless now
one, hold on with love
or let the flames burn it in desire
it belongs just there or nowhere

echoes of silence
echoes of past
the coffee shops
the ice-cream parlour
the autumn gardens
the benches of the grey old class
which reflects the voices till end of time
of ones who sat there
shared love, joy, smile, sorrow, hope and light
walls of present
that rebounds the essence from past
of two sweethearts

she was the burning agony
and he was her coldest desire

because in the end, no matter what, the sun will shine different the next day and the moon will light up the city with some more glory. what do we crave for, the past? people in the past? fairytales? or unknowingly grief. the constant is in our head, contrasts from the variables outside.

like the christmas chronicles
that i longed for
be the glimmering lights that my house craves
or the wishes that bless me
crown me with hopes
and you and faith
take away my winter's curse

for all one knows
she could be that silver in copper
or for one that gold in silver
but for that first love she called
she forever remained his sapphire, despite the
gold he had

'home' is what you call someone
after their welcoming name
perhaps it has lost its meaning
like your heart is now rental
'home' is what you call someone
or maybe just so you never feel out of place
maybe it's where you feel safe
i once cherished the winds that brought us the
morning joy
and the sun that i now hate
that never let the woods grow old
i hate
that now i belong nowhere
although i lie in bits everywhere
because 'home'....
'home' was just a name

it happened in the strangest kind
like the sky and i floated
and the sea sprinkled from above

in the events that were never mine
i found you in the rarest kind
like there you stood a stranger in front of me
and your fine smile that hugged me
your shadow that invited mine
to dance under the summer sun
fate was a work of art
we were closer yet apart

it is a possibility
that we are defined by a million stars
and you say we are out of hope?
~your reach is confined

she said she was sorry
and that it won't happen again
i had to stay
knowing the vastness of mistakes
that will follow
i was familiar with the other path
of how it reached the same end
i knew the epilogue of our story
before another chapter started
after all, i was her hope
she, my love

the old man bent down and tied the little boy's shoe-lace and told him:

son, sometimes it's okay to tie a knot, it's not tangled, it's a knot of simplicity, it won't let you fall.

part 1

i like autumn
hold it together
it makes me wonder a lot
doesn't it make you feel
you find a purpose
but never does it last forever somehow

part 2

my little brother asks me
is love that simple?

asking out on a date
telling she looks nice
making somewhat like vows
spending time till fate's timeline
weekdays, long nights
weekends, long days
a drive, a flower, a song
and hopefully……
it rains

part 3

hold it brother
i beg to differ
quite a nice picture you drew
but like the leaves of autumn
love's a quiver
it's rain, you say
or perhaps water
trying to wash it all away
and your first home will be just one
but many a face and many of a place
what binds two together is more than names

i can't believe you will get to know me like this
through an sms
it means no waiting desperately
for a stranger to drop off my message outside
your house
for knowing what i look like now
thinking if i am having dinner when you are
or worrying if i am back from work by now
everyday naming our future
with no present that's together
we hold hands in letters
and perhaps hug in dreams
what it looks like to have a life on a piece of
crumpled paper
we'll be a paper of art forever it seems

perhaps spring blushed early
and autumn remained a halt for us
summer rained with a ravishing glow
winter melted into thin snow
a perfect kind that you and i crave for

we are always away
from moments of truth
we never know completely what happened
we just call thunder the cause of the wreckage
just a bad time
just a bad day
but there are two sides of a coin
both are exclusively different events
with no blames howsoever
the ~~tail~~ tale differs to an even side
before the assumptions take over

from the wrongs that started me
to the rights
that i'll live for
that was me
i was a poet

we tangled like the finest strings meant to
humm on clashing

when i spend my time
looking at the rushing shore
i wish to hope that you're looking at the blue
patches above
the passion in us that makes us stare
our eyes that talk
and the breath that cares
is the same how the sea talks to the sky
and once again
that makes us no different
you and i

after a decade
i saw her
my wait for this coincidence was over
still like the fresh smell of the rain
your hands held yourself tightly
like you were trying to be safe
i couldn't keep up to the promise i made
it was that rain
that concealed my tears

solitude in the name of you
i was a stranger to the world at once
like a constant stop on the signal
or the butterflies always on the blossom
like a shot
a pullback was you
solitude in the name of you

will i enter your room
and get the idea of you
a guitar lying around
and a distant note of a song
sheets of music in harmony sing of you
or by the gap of curtains
the sun that lights you
will i see a couple of coats lying around
that hides your disguise every time you leave
your guard
a picture of mom and dad in an old frame
will i enter your room and know
you are a lot more than that one place

i have moved on
is finally starting to sound
like i am dying to be found

sometimes i think about the future
will it be like how i imagined it would be?
when that one person comes
will the sky cease to be just sky
but something to float upon and something to
glare
or every blue reminds me of your eyes
or grief will only be the fear now
fear of losing you

it all has to end
but will you make me believe in infinity
i don't want someone to understand me
but someone to be my poetry
and out of all the truths
i crave a fantasy
where music and words and you together in a
line
sometimes i think about the future
i hope my fairytale never turns out to be a lie

when i met the archives
folded papers with dust upon them
pictures of two sweethearts
conversations that had many turns
wrongs that had many rights
it was brutal at some point
as if the alignment disturbed above
and that's when i learnt about love
despite the differences that grew between them
my father did marry my mum
~my child

why is it always till death do us apart and not
i'm the beginning of my story
and the end of yours

sometimes i feel
that i lack the oxygen
reaching all the way within me
maybe this time i give the benefit of doubt
that my heart wants to breathe
not for someone, but for me

flowers are flaws
moon is dark
stars are dying
ocean is vast

and beyond all these facts
someone we know of
makes them all alive, unique, and eternal

earth is emotional, but space is silence, and i know you cannot love the people, but see them fall for each other brings your heart the total warmth. you my love belong to the mesosphere, not close to the earth, not far from the moon either. and maybe that's why i am looking above every time i feel unloved, not the universe, but at you.

and when by all the providence
i found you to be mine

i finally felt
what it's like to hug
the ocean, the universe, the depths, the heights

the quench in me
will die from the passion in your eyes
love in your heart
and i in your mind

with every step closer
i felt the warmth in my heart
that froze the blood in my veins

perfect like an old vine
you walked
gracefully, elegantly
catching everyone's eyes
when you looked right into mine

like the wallflowers
met the roses
it was an impeccable garden

sublime
sə-blīm' - characterised by nobility; of high
moral

can our love be such?
not just in the fine moments but during the
sandstorms too

when they say
let's be eternal in love
it is inexpensive for them
as long as immortality is not a choice

i'd rather live this gesture
than pray for it in another life

so, my dear one
let's be ethereal in love
for we can be presently, delicately, real

i am quieter nowadays
it doesn't feel right to tell someone
i like you
because every time it ends
it does no justice to love
at least one of us should stick to the promise
so, as my precaution
i never talked to anyone new

Stranded in between

Affections and aversions on a single note

.

why did you play the manipulation card
when all you had to do was see
that i was there for you
through your worries as deep as the sea
and my love like shattered leaves
still clinging on beneath a tree
why did you play the manipulation card
when all you had to do was feel

.

first part

it's a shame to say goodbye
to everyone with whom you have ever cried
the red scars we share in the blue seas
that we both got while moving past the broken
reefs

second part

it's a new place without you
where i smell coffee more than ever
and the crowd that suffocates me
i hate being a stranger
because that's all i can be
without you ....

~ *a stranger*

i would never understand consoling
it's definitely not mending

perhaps you find out your fresh wounds
or the inner grief that's been at rest
to be reborn once again
you present an act like i am a fool
you treat them to kill it
you try to make them flee
when you are the craftsman of your own
scarring deeds
~learn to find peace in grief

even amidst the clouds
when i feel closer to the sun
i feel neglected evenly
because the silence lacks peace above
even amidst the blue patches of clouds
somehow

this is trifling
and my soul aches
when me-thought the sky is under heaven's
grace

it breaks my heart to know
what we ask of things while looking above
up here it seems to be like an empty ocean
far cries dispersed into thin air in quick motion
none of rebounds to be expected
for this is the eternal universe
and not the cave that may fulfil your wants

love is typical but not conventional
it is vested in one for
who to love and whom to know

i know you don't remember me
i don't ask you to recall even
but once for me
do visit the heights i called my safe place
do check the lakeside where i talked to eternity
please check my profile to see what i look like
find me drowned in our favourite music
if by chance you manage to find me
i'll give you a dime for what it takes
~i'm not there where i used to be

there's a fear in loving
loving can never scare me
the fear is of losing you
and losing can torment me

hopes and dreams is our ending entity
between i hope you message me
and you dream of calling me
we became the superficial creators
of our never-ending agony
why? because of the trust between the hopes
and dreams
~ *that never came out we imagined it to be*

airports are a hub of fate
if i stand there to see you fly off to another
land
why am i holding myself together by my own
handwhy do my eyes become watery
when you move further away
and why do i shiver with every breath taken
without your scent which was taken away
my concern is concerning
when i wait for that one
to bring themselves out and call out my name
my heart beats that person's name
and still i hold onto their name card
arrivals and departures are the last countdown
flight 6e008 this is your last call
say your goodbyes and call out their names

am i too old and pale to find love unachievable
that i'm smiling at my imagination
~let down by people on a loop

even after sitting by the lakeside for a
thousand time
i couldn't feel the scenery to be mine
for me the water cannot be cold
and the sky cannot push me away
i wish i could and i would be lost between the
valleys i see
or dive, not drown in the depths beneath
i am a lover and preserver
if i find myself shunned
the water in me would cripple into sand

some people are destined to cause emotions to tangle and others meant to suffer. perhaps in another life some scars would be meant to wound one and enough to scare the others away.

now if you call me
i don't want you to recognise me
i always prayed in another life you wouldn't
find me
but i cannot wait any longer
and so, i must let you go
let her go if you love her is a phrase
but i let you go so that i can live once again
my prayers never made you come back to me
so, i pray now to fall even more away
~ *tired of holding on*

back in the summer of 20'
when i used to share music and poems with
you
i never thought
i'll be considering you
to be the tune and the words too

it's been too long of an obsession
and too steep of a depreciation
and when i close my eyes, i happen to know
your name
but never to know what you like
which is worse because
my grief feels like gone in vain
and that's when the obsession ceases
and you seem to be gone for good

cry all you want
not till the paper is wet
but till your heart is dried up

weep all you want
not till you feel drained
but till the anguish feels vacant

because tears can be heavier than snow
and snow can be a thousand rains

for each minute of silence
screams are made on
for every light of hope
clouds are poured upon
and much likely the crave of being loved
grief in invited along

harmony within us
hope within us
home within us
stars within us
and rain within us
that's the bit asked by everyone
but of course, here we are with
strings to tangle us
mistakes to follow us
weather to disrupt us
universe to make us lost
and water to leave us withered within

i am done asking
how have you been?
it's of course not knowing
what goes on in them within
like one can talk to the seashore
and still expect a tide for an answer

i am tired of naming love to be pain
because for once i'd give the benefit of doubt
that even love can be a nameless end of the bay
where no tides follow to take me down
and no wind bears the cold to make me snow
for once when light strikes time down
i'd love to blame the grief
that obstructs my journey to infinity
i am tired of naming love to be pain
because for once
love can be finding you
and heartbreak can be ice too

in the era of
every love language being a thing
will you stay
became the strongest impulse of my being
 *~languages are meant to change, the purpose is
to understand*

you saying, we used to be
i say we had to be
without having to know
i'd not know we were never meant to be

i told you one day that our mind is limitless
but then i also want to say
how i have been feeling the tension
between my neck
how my spine is feeling rigid
and how i am hearing some voices at the back
of my head
how my hands are trembling out of the blue
how my eyes are blurring out my vision too
i have been meaning to tell you
about the pages i have ranted my weariness on
and on the wooden floor on which
i unexpectedly drop off my tears while lying
down
do you still believe what i told you first
that our mind is limitless
if it were it would hold back my overthinking
but my own mind is giving up my body now

to be whole again

a. g. a. i. n.

a – always finding you by mistake
g – gone but never forgotten
a – anticipated my fall but never accepted our
loss
i – inverted how much, our lives
n- never ending rain
and here we go again

in the depths of water
you like to think there's silence merry
but it echoes down there
you are just not ready
to listen to it yet
  ~just like how you meet a wrong person and how
they see the naive heart within you

there are times when i just loathe love
it makes you wonder the fear
and fear the amazements
like always thinking about
if anything is wrong
if something is stopping from being all right
if there's the spark that's gone
or if there was never one to ignite
between the ifs and buts you like that someone
and those are the other times
when faith is in that hidden piece of feelings

i still remember my promise to never tell anyone, anything about you, not when you made me happy, and even a no when you sarcastically hurt me

then there's one time
when all you think about is to be you
or to be the one they like
and that narrows you down
to regret and avalanches
and if by some providence
you make them yours
you fear the person you are to become
yourself? or the one they liked

we all end up in making the list that screwed
us up
but never the reasons that took it all went
away

it's never love
it's never understanding
it's never talking
it's never consoling
it's never promising
it's never never-ending
it's all just expecting

and that's when you are on your anti-clock
hourglass

why is it always
in another life or universe
you would be mine
and not
in another life or universe
i hope to never meet you

we choose to risk grief for happiness
instead of choosing null and void

i'd rather choose the 10 strangers over that one
person
because that one will give me far more
expectations
that the other 10 can ever give me
collectively

i am either the most delusional person or just
someone in love
~acceptance

it's easy to hurt but it's easier to stay, when for
once, you listen to your heart and not the
whisper that your demons unveil.

let me find you a home
a reason to stay
a person to love
a home to name
can you cross your heart
and tell me, this is not something you'll wreck
and then find me to blame

hey kid, you are sixteen, it's like going into the past and telling my younger self this. be wise with love, it's delicate, fragile to words, gestures, mistakes. seems to be one word but it is composed of endless emotions held with delight on situations, regret, patience, forgiveness, mourning, hating, but to all these means, there is one end, and you know that very well mate. it's what you felt, that rush on seeing her, the first one to steal your eyes.

i have written so much about you
but you are so lost in words

i have heard so much about you
but what do you sound like?

i have so many songs that suggest your name
but no lyrics that call you out

i have an album of your pictures in my head
but your name in the gallery says zero photos

perhaps this is the bridge i talked about
between love and pain
and stranded in between

take me with you
take me to the gardens
take me to your favourite ice cream parlour
take me to window shopping
take me to your playlist
take me to your dreams
take me to your safest place
take me to your fearing mind
and take me to your broken heart

from plucking the flowers for you
to mending your heart
take me with you
and i'll take you one step closer to yourself
every hour
~i'm your angel in disguise

either i'm half
or the moon is
on a full moon
i'm an empty heart
~perfect day doesn't exist

the worst part is i missed you all these years
but the thought of having you back hurt more
than that. irrevocable damages are kinder than
invited ones

time to time
you like to take those chances
against all odds like
fire on fire
ice on ice

cut yourself some slack, it's nothing new it's just people, they are meant to hurt, so till the time it's a good time, one has to be kind, satisfied, and peacefully alright. none of your words changed them, it might have been their plan all along. i think that's why it feels right to say to sit back and only care for that next hour, till the moment you are sure, they will stay. and believe this one time, on an hourly basis, there starts a new timeline.

when you shout your name in a cave
you listen to it back again
because it's empty and it reflects evenly

now try calling out yourself to me
don't feel lovable if you hear just your voice
again
i am not only loving you, i am empty from
inside

so, the next time you call out your name
hope that it settles in me

i call forth my deceitful company
i showered upon you my whole of empathy
i protected you like my own house
i burnt the fire in you with my own bare hands
you shoved me off and declared me an enemy
you pretend to take a vile of poison just to
hurt me
you henceforth call my concern
a pitiful and desperate move
what a shame were you
to be the most graceful ending entity

i find it convenient
to look for poetry in someone
as each time, i don't have to find
a new set of words
they all prove to be the clone
of people that i have met before

did it never intrigue you
when i said
i might be falling in love with you

because if it did
then you wouldn't behave this way
like it's my honour and your mistake
you wouldn't make me feel unwanted
and leave me alone
when i say i had a bad day

did it never cross the pathway
in your complicated imagination
to just ask me if i was okay
~it just doesn't feel right anymore

oh how much have you spoiled me
by giving so many affirmations
but also by keeping on to none of them

i am not a lost cause
i am a disturbed one

i read the book you told me to read
i heard the song you shared with me that eve
i ate the food we used to like
i visited the heights where we forgot about our
lives
i did everything that i wrote in my journal
about us
what now? because it was just 'i' in this whole
scene

i preferred the long-term type of love, which had a pinch of all the ingredients except the bowlful of goodbye. every year now, on the second week of june, i make my peace without you. i hold onto you a little, but a bit more i let go of you. my long-term love, gave me an even longer expiration date. the love is in thin air now but the attachment feels like pain.

all i hope is the next week of june is the last. when i make peace without you, i actually feel peaceful after.

actually a goodbye or are we meeting this
saturday to watch the comet that goes by?

fine, you went away
not everything is supposed to work out

but

why did you take my favourite song away?
and why did you take away my safe place?
and my favourite movie?
the pizza that i ordered every time for us
oh, the long drives
the midnight video calls
the nickname that no one else called
the morning of have a nice day
and the goodnight of sleep tight
it's too much of a loss
just because
you went away

belated wishes but why do i take them
better late than never sounds good in movies
because if you had time to post your instagram
stories
i'm sure you had time to message me

keeping your guard up seems good
but why do i see you sweating
and why are you wearing a jacket in this
summer heat
with your gloves worn and mufflers on
~guard up and guard down depends on the
weather called people

now that i am finally making peace with the
high tides
and bringing the silence to the shore
why do i see you ready
to strike the water
with your sword
~is it necessary that one of us has to fight?

hopefully you meet me
when i am helplessly lost

the first time i saw your eyes
i saw a dark brown colour
and then a hint of blue
a line of green
and some hurt in black

when you were out in the world
it was oh so vibrant
in your room
it all went dark

if i am talking to you
when i am out with my friends
and speaking like we are something else
asking about your day
getting you orchids
talking till 4 am

doesn't mean i like you
i'm trying to forget
what it felt to actually care
by lying to myself

i am trusting my instincts
to go in that direction
i am walking on the path
hoping you to be my destination

the last time when they walked together
he knew it was the last time
he will see her
so, he stopped to hug her
he knew, it was a closure

and she,

she accepted it later
that hug was everything they ever wanted

we were the abstract in blacks and whites.

for once let's imagine
we are not the sea and the sky

we are the dark space we talked about at
twilight

you are the mercury
and i will be neptune
and yet we will have our own seas to gaze
and different constellations to stare

you will be brighter than ever
i might be the dullest of all

all i speak to you is
there are entities like the horizon and the
depths of sky
that can bring us like hand and glove
but let's talk when we find a way
to get closer, not merely together
because the point of all this narrows down to
you and i

every time i find someone
i inject some of my pain into them
thinking they'll balance my inner self
so whenever you are trying to look out for me
first take care of yourself

it is generally been prescribed to heal after
moving on. but a part of me is confused, what
if recovery takes away that smile along with
the pain and what if it takes a voice away from
my life, of that one person calling out my
name. what if there is suddenly, one less soul to
think about.
~*just like they never existed*

the only one who knows you in and out
from your first settlement in someone's dreams
to the devastating heartbreak
and the everlasting gut-wrenching feel
it isn't your best friend
or one in your family
it's the songs you heard on loop at 2 a.m.
and the diary you wrote in at 4
the track where you ran to clear your head
and the car you drove in at 154
~sometimes it's not the people who make you feel
better

they don't love you
they don't care
you were their distraction and now they are
yours
except you had the emotions
and they couldn't care less
~reality check is harsh

a thousand strings to tie our knot
each one talking about
something we are
and the latter we are not
i tie it as if making it underneath my shy adore
sewing it concealing my dispersed fragile
thoughts
i am making our fate on needles and threads
what am i to become
your takeaway love
or your deepest regret

journal: 02/03/2022
maybe it is what it is, at the end of the day a
person will be irrational. he or she will look for
a sophisticated companion and then they crave
joy, happiness, fooling around and being
childish and taking that someone as their
home, that is what people want. every other
fantasy that is left in quick succession is what
people take. it's absurd. i will not understand
us humans.
we are all fools.

perhaps

"what love does to you is what loving really is"

"*You pierce my soul, I am half agony, half hope*"
~Jane Austen

ACKNOWLEDGEMENTS

I sincerely present my gratitude to my parents and all those who have helped me to get this book introduced. I hereby collect my last but not the least thoughts and words to extend my love, and respect to my friends and family.

My fellow readers, it was a short journey but I intend to see you soon. Thank you with all my heart for spending your fraction of patience and feelings into this read.

Now I close upon thanking the team for their able support in getting these thoughts all together.

GRATEFUL